Ask Your Way to Success

Ask Your Way to Success

The Definitive Guide to Success Through Asking

How to Transform Your Life by Learning the Art of Asking

Your Path to Success: A Five Part Series

Chase Andrews

Copyright © 2017 by Chase Andrews

All rights reserved. No part of this publication may be reproduced, distributed, or transmitted in any form or by any means, including photocopying, recording, or other electronic or mechanical methods, without the prior written permission of the publisher, except in the case of brief quotations embodied in critical reviews and certain other noncommercial uses permitted by copyright law. For permission requests, write to the publisher, addressed "Attention: Permissions Coordinator," at the address below.

Chase Andrews

chaseandrews@thepassiveincomemachine.com

www.thepassiveincomemachine.com

Make sure to check out the rest of the books in this series:

Fail Your Way to Success: The Definitive Guide to Failing Forward and Learning How to Extract the Greatness Within - Why Failing is an Integral Part of Success and Why You Should Never Fear it

https://www.amazon.com/dp/B0738WDK6W

Discipline Your Way to Success: The Definitive Guide to Success Through Self-Discipline - Why Self-Discipline is Crucial to Your Success Story and How to Take Control Over Your Thoughts and Actions

https://www.amazon.com/dp/B0741FMCBX

Meditate Your Way to Success: The Definitive Guide to Mindfulness, Focus and Meditation - How Meditation is an Integral Part of Success and Why You Should Get Started Now

https://www.amazon.com/dp/B073ZMCHQJ

Believe Your Way to Success: The Definitive Guide to Believing and Your Path to Success How Believing Takes You from Where You are to Where You Want to Be

https://www.amazon.com/dp/B0747N14KF

This book is dedicated to those that are not afraid to ask for the things they truly desire.

Contents

Prologue
- How Asking Fits into the Grand Scheme of Success

Introduction - Asking your way to Success

Chapter 1 Asking, Attracting and Advancing
- Opportunities
- Distractions
- Awareness
- Conscious Awareness
- Mindful Awareness

Chapter 2 Distractions
- Daily Distractions
- Avoiding Distractions

Chapter 3 Opportunities
- Kinds of Opportunities

Chapter 4 Massive Action
- Step 2 Eat Healthily
- Step 3 Balance
- Step 4 Know Your Stuff
- Step 5 Clarity
- Step 6 Keep Moving
- Disciplined Schedule

Chapter 5 Managing Output with Inspiration
- Cultivate Asking
- When in Doubt, Ask
- Just a Few More Steps

Chapter 6 Believing

Conclusion

Epilogue

Prologue

"If you are not willing to risk the usual, you will have to settle for the ordinary"

Jim Rohn

This is the fourth book in a five-part series on success and the acts that must be undertaken before it can be gotten. You will get the best out of this book if you read the entire series but if you are starting here, and this is your first book, it's going to be a powerful introduction to the series. Surely you will benefit greatly if you read all five books in sequence, and also take note to read them repeatedly to get the best out of it.

Success means different things to different people and that is totally understandable. But to get you aligned and revved up, we need to take an unconventional look at success. Let me start by telling you what it's not. Success is not the small achievements you have when getting that promotion or buying that dream car. Success is serious business. If you want to really attain it and experience it consistently, not just being a one-hit wonder, you need to redefine the filters that you see yourself with.

You are the embodiment of potential. Each and every part of you, without exception, is the personification of all that is needed to impact this world and upgrade it to a better version of itself. Visualize this: The other day someone sent me a link showing a time-lapse video of the Earth as taken from a geosynchronous satellite. In it, the earth transitioned through night and day a number of times. True beauty could be seen in the movement of the clouds, the rising and setting of the sun, and most amazing sight was seeing the lights come up at night. You could, from space, see all the populated areas lighting up. With such a breathtaking sight, I couldn't help but think of how Edison had touched this world and how much his inspiration, his toils, his failures, and his belief passed from his lifetime and into ours. To be able to see cities glow at night, because one man wouldn't give up, is an amazing experience.

Success is what we do in this physical world that adds to it. It is not something that we can do on our own. We need to be truly inspired. Success is not about copying something or mimicking something else. It's not about just combining two ideas and making a new one. All those things may be good sometimes, but you are much more capable of doing greater and that is where true success is birthed.

To be able to succeed, you need to attract the universe and be a conduit for it. That's what being human means - to be a conduit between the intangible energy that makes up the universe and the physical reality we exist in. You have to pluck the ideas from the intangible and bring it to life here in the tangible world.

If you want to be successful, you must want it and this means that you have to ask for it. You must attract it with all your being and then it will come. It won't come pre-packaged and shiny; of course not. This isn't a game show where you win stuff out of sheer dumb luck. This is reality. Here, you have to ask for it and when the universe responds to your request, it presents an opportunity. You have to take that opportunity and do something with it. That's how you make success.

How Asking Fits into the Grand Scheme of Success

Sometimes, we take the importance of asking for granted and we take success for granted as well. I will strongly advise you to stop doing that and take both very seriously. Success is serious business and asking, while seeming trivial, underscores the aligning of the resources and forces that bring about the success that you aim to achieve. The 'how's and the why's' of the process of asking will be explained in further chapters of this book. For now, you just need to know that asking, along with virtues like discipline, meditation, failing and believing, are critical to your level of perseverance over the course of your life. With this understanding, you can begin to lay the new foundation that consists of the five following elements.

- The first is the ability to understand failure, and how failure can lead to success.
- The second is to recognize and internalize discipline so that when your inspiration demands shifting into high gear and bringing forth massive action in which your body will do as your mind commands. The first two books set the stage for success; what it means; and why you shouldn't short-change yourself as to the height of your success.
- The third is the power of meditation that you need to understand your place and purpose in the world so that you can go on to leverage who you are and make your meditation bear fruits.
- The fourth element, that is needed, is the ability to ask and a strong grasp and understanding of what to ask for.
  People are often astounded by how simple the notion of asking really is. We sometimes

choose not to ask, because subconsciously, we are not ready for success, or we are in fear of it. If you can't ask for success, then it should occur to you that there is some form of baggage that you need to jettison, and that needs to be taken care of by means of meditation and reflection. Asking is an art that you need to internalize. As simple as it sounds, many people lose the ability and the inclination to ask for what they want even though they may want to. Asking is needed in both the start of your journey and its proceeding course. Whatever you ask for, the Universe will grant.

- Finally, there is the element of belief. You need to believe that anything and everything is possible. You need to believe that what you will embark on will yield a positive result in the making of your success and the reaching of your greatness.

This series on success gives you the information you need to find the potential in you and to achieve the success that you are born to get. The material is laid out in five books, ideally, read in sequence.

i. Fail Your Way to Success
ii. Discipline Your Way to Success
iii. Meditate Your Way to Success
iv. Ask Your Way to Success

v. Believe Your Way to Success

You must approach this book and the rest in this series with an open mind. After all, what have you got to lose? If you've tried everything else and you are not getting the success that you know is within you, it's time to change your perception (how you see things), how you approach things and how you move things.

To approach the gates of success in its entirety, you will have to lay assault on the hordes of ignorance multiple times, reflect on the meaning of success, and weed out the negative mindset that has prevented you from the things that you need to embrace. You will be surprised to see how the same lines can have a deeper impact each subsequent time you come at it until you get to a point that the information becomes fluid and your own truth emerges from it.

Introduction - Asking your way to Success

There are two sides to the coin of existence and, as with all coins; one side cannot exist without the other. On one side of the coin, you have all things that are tangible. We call this *'phenomenon'*. And on the exact opposite side of it, we have the intangible which we call *'noumena'*. The terms were first coined and put to use in this reference by philosopher Immanuel Kant. We are not going to dive too deeply into Kantian philosophy here although we will borrow some of his ideas to solidify our point as we move along.

If you look at the fundamentals of this existence and all things built from it, you will come to the realization that all things that flow from life also mimic its duality of *phenomenon* and *noumena*.

In the mid 350 BC, somewhere north of today's Greece, in the town of Pella, a child was born to Philip II of Macedon and Olympias of Epirus. They named him Alexander and this young prince went on to replace his father as King when he was just 21. His kingdom was small, but his ambitions were gargantuan. By the time this king was 34, he died of mysterious causes. But in that short 13 year period which he reigned, he had become one of the wealthiest men in the world, conquering all the lands stretching from the Bosporus to the Hindu Kush. His military genius earned him the title of 'Alexander the Great', and in some places, he was worshiped as the heir of Zeus.

Putting aside all the military tactics and leadership skills this young man had, his major personal trait that was impressed on me was his belief in a higher power. Of course, the description of the higher powers back then were all personifications of the Grecian gods and goddesses, and we can sit here all day to debate the theology of pagan religions, but that's not the point. The thing that stuck me in all the history that I've read about this amazing man was the fact that he would rely on two things besides his small army.

The first was his reliance on some form of meditation; the second was his ability to launch massive action in whatever he was doing. Whether it was quelling the rebellion in Greece, or laying siege on kingdoms that resisted him or attacking his nemesis, the Persian Empire. Meditation and massive action always led to the success that Alexander was famed for.

In his pattern and as well with others that had arrived on the success stage before and after him, you will notice that success is made of two parts. One part *phenomenon* and the second is *noumenon*. There is always a tangible side that comes together with an intangible side when success is contemplated. Not all of it comes with meditation as the manifestation of the intangible. Asking is a form of intangible, especially when the asking is done in the form of vibrations that you transmit to the universe. Learn to ask for anything and everything: ask for inspiration, ask for solutions to an intractable problem, and ask for ideas. You can ask for anything, and if you can strike the right vibration in your asking, the answer will come.

When you combine asking with massive action, the results are nothing short of spectacular.

***

Chapter 1 Asking, Attracting and Advancing

Your conscious mind is at the center of all the things you do and all the things that you want to do. That is your natural mode of communication and the traffic cop that regulates what you do at any point in time. What do I mean by traffic cop? Well, for most of us who have yet to internalize and advance our ability to remain in a state of mindfulness and meditation 24/7, we are directed and controlled by the commands of our conscious mind, save for the situations where we are overwhelmed or where we are taken off our stride. Our conscious mind retains control over most of our thoughts and actions and it does so by the means of a language that it seems to whisper in our inner ear.

You've heard this language at numerous occasions and still, we take for granted the fact that this is the voice that we should be listening to in almost all the things we do and all the things we think about. But it should not be - at least it should not be the one if we are serious about becoming successful beyond the wildest dreams of almost everyone we know personally.

That voice is the speech issued from the conscious mind and it has its good days and bad days. Our first step should be the ability to recognize when it has its good days and when it is undergoing its terrible moments.

Our second step would be to change the way those bad days manifest so that our conscious mind learns how to flip out of a bad day and sail along smoothly as it would on good days.

You may have noticed that there are some days where think you are invincible. You feel like you can take on anything and anyone and come out a winner: nothing can get you down. These are, of course, your good days.

Then, there are the bad days, or 'not-so-good' days, where you know the moves, but you just can't get your feet in sync or you just can't get the words to come out right. You feel like a bumbling buffoon. Trust me: you are not the only one. We all have those days. For some of us, it's more of those days that occur than the good ones, and for others, it's less of those days that comes and more of the good ones. As logic dictates, the people who have fewer of those bad days and more of the good days are going to be the ones with a higher probability of success and take a shorter course to achieving greatness.

Remember Alexander the Great? - well he must have had a lot of those good days because a bad day on the battlefield is one where you don't walk away victorious and since he achieved what very few men achieved - conquering most of the known world in less that twelve years, he most certainly had more good days than anyone else I know.

However, I don't think that success just randomly came to him, I am pretty sure he had to work hard at it; Just like how I had to work at constantly transforming my terrible moments into great times and recognizing those bad feelings before they manifested in my actions.

Recognizing the bad days is a key part of you being able to align the forces that can make things happen for you.

Why? If you are not having a great day, whatever you are about to ask for or whatever you are about to work on, are not going to be tainted by something that can actually be controlled.

The best way to begin is to be vigilant in your current state at all times. If you are aware of your present condition then you can do whatever it takes to get your bad days fixed and get to achieving success. The best way to remain aware of your present condition is to be in a constant state of mindfulness regardless of the distractions that come across your path.

As you advance through your daily tasks, there is potential for numerous distractions to come your way. The challenge is that these distractions sometimes can be disguised as opportunities. Just by stopping to evaluate them can sometimes throw you off track. This means that you have to be careful with what may seem like good potential. But then, the question that arises is how do we recognize potential opportunities? The answer to that, and the previous concern about being distracted, is the same. If you can fine-tune your state of mindfulness in all the things that you do, what you will be left with is the instantaneous ability to sidestep distractions yet recognize opportunities.

One point that you need to understand about opportunities and distractions is that seeming opportunities that are out of sequence with your task at hand are actually distractions. If you are in the midst of doing something yet the thought or event that props in front of you seems like an opportunity for something else, you should walk away from it.

Opportunities

A separate discussion of opportunities is a worthy departure from the main subject of the book. As you can see, there are opportunities and there are distractions. Opportunities that are not in sync with your current tasks and have no benefits whatsoever to you, are distractions. But opportunities that advance your objective are real opportunities.

There is only one source where opportunities emanate from and that is the universe. You have to attract the opportunities you need and not leave it to chance. In fact, the only place that opportunities are left to chance is in your conscious mind. Everything that you ask for will show up at some point. Remember that saying, "***Be careful what you ask for, you might just get it.***"? Well, it's incorrect. There is no "might" about it. Whatever you ask for, you will get. So, indeed, you need to be careful what you ask for because when it comes, it could be distraction. How can an opportunity be a distraction? Well, I can see how that can be confusing. Opportunities can be distractions because they do not further or advance your current task that is designed to fulfill your inspiration.

It becomes a problem because it takes you away from doing something that you are in the midst of doing while not adding value to it. This happens because your mind has asked for the second opportunity and so the universe has granted it. Indeed you can be the cause of your own distractions. You will not have these kinds of distractions if you keep your mind focused on the tasks and objective at hand and that is part of the reason why you should read how to meditate yourself into success.

Every opportunity you get is because you asked for something that relates to it in some form. Opportunities don't just show up. You have to ask for them. Whatever you ask for will come to you because the universe hears everything that you ask for when you are in a certain state and it responds by aligning the opportunities for you to take.

There have been many instances in my life where I have been careless with what I asked for. The result was that I got every single one of them and they were not all as good as I thought they would be.

Many of you will misunderstand this part about asking for things and getting the opportunity. When you ask for something on a whim, you will get it, and when the opportunity comes, you look at it and you are torn by what to do. There is only one thing to do, let it go. But the next time teach yourself to be cognizant of what you ask for.

On the other hand, if you are constantly focused on one area and you are constantly asking for all that relates to that goal, then the opportunities that you get will be related to it. When you combine your mindful state to the things that you ask for, then what you get are the puzzles of the picture that you are looking to assemble.

Success is made more efficient if you ask for things that you are mindful of. The asking is done in a different frequency than just opening your lips and muttering a voice, it is done instead by a vibration in your soul. But you must be able to verbalize at least part of it. If not, it is almost certain that you have no idea what you are asking for. The ability to ask and your act of asking tend to align your conscious and subconscious to the point that your entire soul vibrates in unison.

This is the key to asking, and that forms the basis of your ability to succeed in any area you need to.

It's not about repetition where you keep asking for the same thing over and over again. Have you tried doing this? I have. And it doesn't work unless somewhere along the line you are vibrating it out to the universe and it comes true. You may think it's the repetitive asking that's making it happen. It's not. It's the vibration you are sending out to the universe.

But there is one aspect that you can do physically to be able to move this along. You must be able to ask for it in a cogent and real manner in your conscious mind. Your ability to sound it out and be able to vibrate from hearing it will take you much further than the blind repetition of it.

Have you ever heard a song or a piece of music that just gets you going? You feel the inspiration and you feel the vibration. That's a form of vibration that gets you in the right zone. That zone and state of being are like a tuning fork that hits the right note and when you transmit, it's like a carrier wave on a radio transmitter. It goes straight out to the universe and the law of attraction pulls you towards your goal and pulls your goal towards you.

You are then given the opportunity to make things happen and make things into what you want them to be.

That is the asking that you need to enforce and that is the kind of asking that will make a difference in your life.

Distractions

Distractions, veiled or otherwise, are very different from opportunities but they feel like the same thing. That is why they are insidious. You think they are there to help you but what they will do is drag you backward. The skill you need to develop is to be able to identify them and discard them.

The desire to distinguish between the two, opportunities and distractions, is the point where you need to begin. You have now realized that opportunities that seem innocuous and even acceptable may actually be a distraction. You have also now come to realize that distractions have various kinds. There are those distractions that are pure distractions. They can be events that appeal to your vanity; appeal to your laziness; appeal to your desires in different ways - all the while distracting you from your ultimate goal and the path to your success.

These are the distractions that are easily identified. You just need to stop for a moment and realize that they are keeping you from your path. Seems easy enough, right? You just need to do it.

There are three things you need to be aware of and when you keep them percolating at the back of your mind, then you are going to be able to stave off any of these distractions.

First, you need to remember that you have dual purposes. One is the purpose of your body to make sure that you live. That is your physical body's primary purpose and you read about this in the previous book in this series, '*Discipline Your Way To Success*'. In that book, you learned that we are all endowed with dual purposes. The body, with its feelings; and pleasures and pains are all channeled with the purpose of keeping itself alive. When you feel the pangs of hunger, you are taught to reach for food. That food is designed to give you nutrition and give you nourishment.

The body is the seat of the soul - an energy that is connected to the universe, from where you draw your inspiration. That soul has a different purpose which is to lift you to greatness; that kind of greatness that you've seen in the people that have achieved it before us.

The likes of Martin Luther King, Mother Theresa, Winston Churchill, and Abraham Lincoln – are inspired men and women who knew, in the depths of their souls, the purpose they had to fulfill. Each of them succeeded in rising to greatness and with their greatness showered us all with the ability to dream and see the way to a better existence.

The second form of distractions is our dual selves. We've seen how we have the corporal part of us desiring to live and procreate: then there is the soul in us that is desirous and built to do great things. However, one keeps distracting the other and we almost always give in to the one with the more powerful tool - the body.

The key is to align both towards the same direction and that requires discipline. We talked about discipline in the third book in the series, *Discipline Your Way To Success*.

But before you can do that, you have to identify certain things as distractions and other things as opportunities. In this part of the book, we are going to talk about the distractions within us. As you can infer by now, the distraction that we are talking about here is the distraction that occurs because of the dual purposes. When the body needs to do the things that it needs to fulfill its purpose, you see that it distracts the mind from doing what the soul needs to fulfill its purpose. On the other hand, when the soul is going gangbusters on getting its purpose done, it sometimes forgets to do what the body needs to fulfill its purpose.

The balance that you strike between doing both is one that makes or breaks your efforts. If you pay too much attention to the soul's objective, you may end up being unhealthy, you may neglect your family, you may just break the chain of your life or the growth of your progeny. At the same time, if you get so involved in keeping up with the body's pleasures and objectives, you might get sidetracked from the soul's objectives.

The key is to know where you are and what you are doing. The key is to not give in to habits that change the balance and the key is to be able to be aware of what you are doing so that in the event you get carried away by any one or the other you are able to pull yourself back and get back to fulfilling both objectives.

To be able to fulfill your soul's advance to greatness, you need to be able to have a body to take you there.

If you want that legacy to continue you need progeny to carry that on. If you neglect the purpose of your body, you will not get too far with your soul's objective.

On the other hand, if you neglect your soul and focus only on the desires of your body, then you are not going to be able to fulfill your soul's objective as well.

The only way you can advance forward and fulfill your soul's greatness is to be able to fulfill your dual purposes and recognize the distractions that one throws up against the other. The way to do that is to bring on stage one more asset that you have that you don't really talk about. That is your mindset of awareness.

If you have a mindset of awareness you will start to be totally aware of what is going on and how it's going, and even be aware of the road that leads to inefficient combinations. The point that you will slowly start to see is that you need balance in all you do. But it's not a 50/50 balance. You need to find the balance that gives you the best utility. And if you ask for that, to know your limits and to know your abilities, what you will slowly start to see is the balance that you can extract and move forward in the most powerful of ways.

Awareness

Most people have a wrong idea of awareness. They think that merely knowing they exist is the same thing as being aware. It's not.

Being aware is more than that and it takes practice and experience, especially since most of us are totally unclear as to what it feels like to be aware of ourselves. One of the greatest things about being human is the ability for us to be aware of our existence and to be aware of questions that we do not have the answer to. That is the beginning of all learning. We are able to realize that there are some things we do not know, and in fact, the smarter you are the more you realize that there is a lot more you do not know. Only a fool goes down the path thinking that they know everything.

But there is a difference between those who are aware and those who are not. There is the limit to awareness that you need to be aware of and exceed that limit by invoking other areas of your existence. For instance, you can only be consciously aware of a number of areas in this universe. But beyond that, it doesn't work. The parallel to this is the five senses. If you were to think that all there is to know in the universe is the extent of what you can detect with your five senses then you are going to miss out on all of the truths that are out there. For instance, you would be oblivious to infrared and thereby not clear as to how the remote control works. For all you know, it's some form of dark magic. But since you are more consciously aware of something called infrared - a wave of frequency that is beyond any of your senses to detect - you are now able to know that this is not black magic, but one of the electromagnetic frequencies of the universe.

In the same way, this applies to physical items, there are things that do not apply. In the early days of science, scientists were expounding as fact, that space was a void. Only much later did we realize that there are other forms of energy and matter that are in space, we are just not able to detect and make sense of it.

Conscious Awareness

Conscious awareness is very different from mindful awareness. They can intersect and we can choose to live our lives in this intersection but before that, we need to understand the difference and the way each is used.

Conscious awareness is when you understand entirely what something is and you are aware of its existence so much so that when any of your senses pick it up, you know what it is and where it comes from and how it affects you. Take for instance the smell of smoke from a fire. If you were to sense it, you will instantly be aware of it. You may also be triggered to realize that there is impending danger. This is conscious awareness. You know exactly what something is and you know when it presents itself.

Mindful Awareness

On the other hand, there is the mindful awareness. Mindful awareness is one where you do not necessarily need your senses to detect it. You are in a state that you know what is happening at a level that is beyond your consciousness. Sometimes this is thought to be the subconscious. There is nothing wrong with that, but remember that mindful awareness is about you being able to know and understand your immediate space and time deeply.

By practicing mindful awareness, what you end up doing is keeping tabs of what is constantly going on with you, in you, around you and within you. But what you are not concerned with is the past or what happens next. Your only concern is to be able to be in the moment.

The funny thing about the moment is that it is the quality of the moment that yields a better result. Not the multitasking moment that you think can be more productive. It is not productive at all to do multiple things at once, and in fact, it is counterproductive.

Nobel Laureate Rabindranath Tagore writes in one of his poems:

"The butterfly counts not months but moments and has time enough.

Time is a wealth of change, but the clock in its parody makes it mere change and no wealth".

He articulately tells us that the life of a butterfly is short in comparison but yet it has time enough to understand life and live its entire lifetime it that span.

Being aware in our own life makes us like that butterfly. Aware we are able to live a lifetime in that moment even though we are not concerned with the past or the future - only the present. That sort of awareness may seem illogical, but it is proven time and again that if you arm yourself with that kind of awareness you will be able to move mountains and rivers to your desire.

He also says that time is a wealth of change and that change, and how much of it we can structure, is the measure of our wealth. Not one of these can be merely done by our hands with mindless motion or done at the instruction of a mind that is not inspired by the soul. True success cannot come about from these menial steps. True success comes from the inspiration that instructs the mind and the mind that converts it to physical action by the hand.

Awareness is a simple enough a measure to do. While you practice mindfulness and reach your awareness, you will be able to know where you are and what to ask for so that your next step can be in the right direction.

The more you can be aware, the more you will be able to accomplish in that moment of time. Just like the butterfly that has only a short time but has enough moments, you have to realize that success is a function of how effective you are at bringing the three resources that you have at your disposal. Your soul, your mind, and your body are the three resources that, when you combine, can make wonders. It can send men to the moon and other planets. It can make devices that harvest the sun's energy for conversion to other devices. It can do almost anything. The key to all this is your state of awareness and the alignment of the three resources.

The idea of asking for something is for you to be able to align your three resources. When you do not ask, you are not aligning it as you should. Your soul may be going in one direction, your body may be going in another and your mind may be trying to figure the next step. When all three forces are pointing in opposing directions, your net movement is, either very slow and indeterminate, or completely stagnant.

By asking, you align and make all parts aware of one true intention. The key then is to iron out what that true intention should be. If that true intention is earthly in nature, then the outcome would be suboptimal. We use the term earthly to describe the desires of the body. To live, to have a family and to enjoy the fruits of the labor you have put in. These can get out of hand very quickly. The idea, while seeming to be to abstain from all sorts of fun, is not really the point. However, the way to do it is to be aware of how much fun you are having and to curtail it the moment it starts to distract from your united purpose.

That is the power of awareness. If you can then take that mindful awareness and conjoin it to the conscious awareness, then what you have is a powerful communication of purpose and abilities. You can't do much with just the desires of the soul, and you can't do much with just the desires of the body, but once you combine them, things start to happen for you.

Awareness is the key to understanding where you are and to keep you in line with the moment that makes you whole. Wholeness is about the joining of your mind, body, and soul. That is the power to succeed. When you keep this in balance, you feed all three. You feed the soul with meditation, you feed the mind with intellect and you feed the body with health. What you end up having is an unstoppable force that will deliver success time and again without any cause for doubt that you will ever miss a beat.

Action comes from the body and from the direction of the mind. Action is the penultimate in the journey. It takes you from inspiration to reality. Each fruit of your action is the end of the journey that you gain in making what inspiration gave you in the beginning.

What we are most addicted to in terms of the body is action. We are so caught up with movement that you need to realize that sometimes you end up moving without making any movement. In this case what we are talking about is the movement that is without direction. The movement without direction and thought, and the thought without inspiration, is a waste of energy. It is a distraction and will not get you anything for your troubles.

To advance, you need your action to be instinctive and well thought out. The part of you that needs to think about the consequences of your actions and keep you moving is that part of you that needs to be driven by the understanding of purpose and the understanding of your limitations.

So when you ask, you start by asking for the identification of those limitations and the rectification of those limitations. Your limitations are not really limitations if you know how to manage them. Limitations are merely misplaced strengths. You just need to know where to put them in order to extract the best value from them. Think of it this way. Have you ever played with a jigsaw puzzle as a child? I have.

I use to enjoy putting up 1000-piece puzzles as a kid and then on to 5000-piece puzzles. Watching the picture take shape was such a thrill for me. Life is like that. Everything that you have in you is like a piece of the puzzle in the box. If you take a piece and try to fit in the wrong place, it's not that the piece is a weakness; it's just that the piece is in the wrong place.

In the same way, if you have a weakness, then you are just misplacing your strengths. When you are aware of yourself and your soul, then you will spend less time trying to put the wrong pieces in the right place. You will be able to align the pieces in such a way that they fall into place and you would be able to achieve your greatness with less frustration and pain.

That is about all there is to get it right. Anytime you get something wrong, just put the pieces back in the box and find the part of you that goes in the right place. That is all there is to it.

Advancing your life is about taking advantage of all your resources and putting them together so that you are able to move the inspiration you have from the depths of your soul and make them appear in front of you. The next step for you to do is understand that asking aligns all those that you need, and when you are aligned you can make magic.

***

Chapter 2 Distractions

We talked about distractions in the last chapter to give you an introduction to the two similar events that will happen in your life. The first was distractions that come disguised as opportunities. The second form of distractions we talked about were the distractions that the body gives the soul and the distractions the soul gives the body by virtue of their sometimes competing purposes. There are many times that the body's purpose to live is a distraction the soul's purpose of achieving greatness.

But distractions are more than just that. Distractions can come in the form of misaligned strengths and even misaligned intentions, and the only way to prevent that is to be aware of your place and aware of your state.

The only foolproof way of being immune to distractions is that you practice mindfulness on a constant basis and if you remain aware of your surroundings and of yourself at all times. There is nothing wrong in feeling aware of yourself in the moments that you feel weakness, or in the moments you feel strong. There is nothing wrong in knowing exactly what you are capable of and what you are not. These kinds of awareness are problematic if you allow your ego to come into play. With the ego in play, you will tend to block your ability to do anything that is able to keep you aware. That is the real reason ego is not a great ally.

If you want to stay aware of your condition and situation, you need to first and foremost remove all vestiges of your ego. Doing that may be simple to a few, but to most, it is one of the hardest things to do because there is a wholesale misunderstanding of what the ego is and what humility in its opposition can be. Humility is always taken as the opposite of the manifestation of ego, but that is not always right. In this case, we are talking about the ego that distracts you from being able to listen to the inspiration you need and do the things that are necessary to succeed in the tasks you have at hand.

What do we mean by ego in this situation? Ego is the over importance of self that concerns the consciousness with looking superior and being self-important. There are those who misunderstand the part of the self-importance so let's clarify that.

When you board a plane, and if you are carrying a young child or baby, you will be advised that in the event of rapid decompression that you should first reach for and don the oxygen masks on yourself. Not your baby or your young child, but for yourself. Why? Because if you don't take care of yourself and you pass out from the rapid decompression, you will not be able to save the baby and don his or her mask and that could be fatal for the child. So even though you have a duty to look after that child, you have to look after yourself to be able to look after him or her. That self-preservation or care for yourself can be described as self-importance and thus a subset of the ego, but it's not.

You have to take care of yourself and you have to preserve yourself for the purpose of being able to take care of your purpose in life. In other words, it's the same as the balance between body and soul. If you do not take care of your body, you will not be able to be of much use to the soul.

So to get back to the ego, here is what you need to do and understand. You need to be able to look after and reward your body, within reason, for the effort it takes in doing what it does so that you can go further and do what the soul needs. To that extent, there is no distraction in the needs of the body and needs of the soul.

But when you go past that line and the needs of the body are merely to extract the pleasure from the actions that please the body, then you are starting down the slippery slope. Your intention and how you discharge your actions can be a distraction to what you need to accomplish from the perspective of the overall purpose.

Asking for this alignment and this balance is a good place to start. This way you will minimize potential for distraction and that will save you time and resources in the pursuit of success.

Daily Distractions

We all face distractions on a daily basis. I face them in the work I do, and I face them in the form of noisy neighbors, traffic jams, annoying sounds. All kinds of things can be distracting if you allow them to be. Over time, I have found that there are many ways you can sidestep distractions just by asking for what you want. If you can't set your desire to a simple sentence that is specific enough to have it beat at the heart of the matter, then you really haven't got your purpose or your direction sorted out. That is the best way to meander through life and succeed at nothing.

To be able to set your daily distractions in perspective, ask for the guidance to be able to look past distractions. I find that mindfulness helps with this as well. By being mindful I have found that I am able to move past errant sounds and noises. I find that I am not distracted by distractions because when I ask for the strength I need I somehow find it.

When you align your body, mind, and spirit to one goal, that goal becomes all the easier to accomplish and it becomes easier to do it each successive time you are faced with the distraction. I align my body, mind, and spirit by daily meditation that is not just designed to calm me down but to help me in sidestepping distractions.

The ability to change your predicament, from one that is in the midst of distractions to one that is free from them, will rely on two factors. The first is that you need to recognize your situation. The second is that you need to be able to change those distractions by ridding them from your path or moving around them.

Avoiding Distractions

There are three ways you avoid distractions. The first is by the use of discipline. You look at a distraction straight in the eye, you steady your footing and you deny its existence. Sounds fancy, but how does that work?

For it to work, you have to be honest with yourself. You need to know exactly what you are going after and when something else comes along, you need to be able to walk away from it. When you use discipline you temper your excitement of a seeming opportunity and choose instead to do what you are already doing and see it through to completion.

The second way for you to avoid distractions is that you be very clear in the desires that you transmit to the universe. For this to happen, you need discipline in what you ask for, instead of just discipline against being distracted after the opportunity presents itself.

Finally, the third way you can avoid distractions is to master the art of mindfulness, focus, and meditation that you are in a constant state of control. You know exactly what is happening around you and what is going on in the veil of the seeming opportunity.

As you start identifying the various distractions that come along, you will be able to recognize them with better facility in time. It takes practice after knowing the theory.

The distractions that we have talked about all this while are distractions that are related to opportunities. They do not address the distractions that are completely unrelated to your life. You may have distractions that arise in your personal life. You may have distractions in terms of emergencies and you may have distractions in terms of weaknesses. These distractions aren't really distractions they are stumbling blocks.

The thing about stumbling blocks is that I have found them to be opportunities to grow. You can either trip over a block and call it a stumbling block or you can arrange the blocks and use them to climb higher. How you use them is up to you.

***

Chapter 3 Opportunities

The main thing you need to know about opportunities is that they are a gift from the universe. It is through opportunities that you receive all the wealth and successes you hope for. If you are expecting gold nuggets to fall from the sky, then you are going to be sorely disappointed. It never works that way.

How it does work is by you asking for something in execution of your inspiration, and by the laws of attraction, you will attract the opportunity that allows you to make what you need.

It's as simple as that. If you've heard stories of people wishing and asking for wealth and cars and jets and it appeared one day, those are mere fairy tales and I do not believe a single word of it because everyone I know has fulfilled their inspiration and became successful by working with the opportunities that were given to them - including yours truly, who is currently penning these words.

In the beginning of the book, I mentioned the balance between *phenomena* and *noumena* - the two sides of the same coin of life that balances the tangible with the intangible. It works here brilliantly as well. The intangible is the vibration that you create when you ask for what you desire. The universe responds with lots of opportunities. You then need to work at it with tangible action to create that result. That is the simple chain of events and it works across the board.

The pairing of tangible and intangible go across every stage of the arc of success and you will get used to it in time and practice. I have also observed in myself, in friends close to me, and in other successful people that the sequence of success gets faster and quicker resulting in an accelerated series of success as you go from one to the next.

Now lets examine the types of opportunities that the universe presents to us.

Kinds of Opportunities

You need to understand a number of things when it comes to opportunities. There are three kinds of opportunities that you will be faced with;

- The first is the most promising and it is the one that is relevant to the work you have at hand. It is most relevant because it is what you need at that point in time. The more focused and mindful you are, and the more aware you are of the circumstances in front of you, the more you will automatically attract the solutions to it in the form of opportunities. When these opportunities arrive, there will be no confusion on your part. It is almost like putting together a jigsaw puzzle and reaching into the box and finding the exact piece you need at the exact moment. These are the situations that you find yourself with if you are totally in a state of mindful awareness in the things that you are doing.

- The second kind of opportunity that will present itself in the event that you are not mindful and only semi-aware of your present state and partially aware of the task, is that you will be inviting other types of opportunity and many a time, you will not be able to tell if they are the right opportunities for the task at hand. You may even be unable to recognize the relevant or real opportunity that is best for the current task, and that would cost you in terms of time and mistakes. This can be frustrating, and energy consuming.

Just remember, an opportunity that does not advance your current purpose is not an opportunity no matter how good it looks.

The failures you encounter in the wake of these moments are designed to do one of two things; you are to either learn the physical errors that arise from these misguided opportunities, or you are meant to wake up and realize that you are not aware of what you are doing. You need to get out of the current state that you are in and put yourself into a position of full awareness to be able to get what you are doing to come out well.

- The third kind of opportunity is not really an opportunity. It is really a full-blown distraction that is clothed in opportunity's apparels. The seeming opportunity is something that totally distracts you from what you are doing and makes you question your resolve. It seems as though the new opportunity is better than the one you are working on. This is the most insidious of all so-called opportunities. It almost feels like you are given the opportunity to move on to something better in the midst of doing something in the present. In actual fact, you will never be able to exit the cycle of zero accomplishment.

In many cases, you are in this position because you have almost zero inspiration and you are not communicating with the universe, which is what you really need. You are not aware of your desire and you are not aware of your actions. This kind of an opportunity has only one good benefit that comes with it; which is the warning that you are at the point of being truly lost.

If you are getting opportunities out of nowhere and they are not the opportunities you desired, move on. Move away from the things that do not fit your goal or your aspirations and return to a state of mindfulness and focus. You need to be able to redirect your energies toward your inspiration.

The third form of opportunities is merely telling you that you need to get in touch with your inspiration, and to do that, you need to be able to find a way to become aware of yourself and your existence. The only way I know how is by mindfulness and focus. It's one of the topics discussed in this series on Success.

***

Chapter 4 Massive Action

Up till this point, we've been majorly discussing about the 'how to attract what you need' and 'what you want'. In the later part of the book, we will return to it in order to show you some of the things that you need to do to be able to get to the point of achieving success.

For now, we are going to turn our attention towards the action that needs to follow your inspiration and the way to go about performing such action. Once again, if you look back to the *phenomena* and *noumena* principle, you will find that attracting the opportunity is the noumena - the intangible. But making it work is the phenomena. The phenomena that is required to make things happen is the massive action that you need to take on a daily basis. You have to be ready to get up early and hit everything you are designed to do really hard.

This chapter is called massive action and that's not a mistake or an exaggeration. You need to be able to do the physical work to get what you are going after. We will start from the bottom up and take things step by step in preparation for taking massive action. But before we start, let's examine the reason why you are taking massive action in the first place. Purpose, they say, precedes existence, and if the purpose of a certain course of action is not clearly stated, abuse would be a constant stop in the path.

When you are inspired and ready, the opportunities that come to you are exactly what you need to make things move and make things happen. There is no doubt in that. Once you are totally in sync and, as they say, *can walk through rain drops*, you are in the zone and you are attracting exactly what you need, this is the time you should remove any barrier to your hesitation and you should just go all out. Do not even stop for one moment because that's just a waste of time. My mother used to tell me this all the time, and she used to invoke the old saying, "*Strike while the iron is hot.*"

You do not want to waste any time. Trust me on this.

Get moving. Once you are in the zone, you put pedal to the metal, you push it up to full throttle and you get going. You don't stop for anything or anyone.

The only question at that moment is, Can your body can keep up?

That brings us to the first step in massive action.

Step 1 Massive Workouts

As the title suggests, you need to work out and get your body in shape. The two kinds of workouts you need are; endurance and strength training. If for some reason you are unable to run, you can begin cycling. If you are unable to cycle - and what I mean by being unable is that you are physically challenged, you should use your wheelchair and you should push yourself for endurance buildup. You need to extract two things from massive workouts;

The first is that you need to find the limits of your body and push them further - expand your body's ability to go further. Every day and every week, you should be able to expand your body's ability to do more and more. This not only creates a better and more physical you - which your body is going to reward you for, it is also going to teach you the power of resistance.

As you expand your limits in workout sessions, your body starts to understand who the boss is and the body is going to start to listen to you because, in time, it starts to realize that you know what you are doing since the body is getting healthier and better.

You also start to feel different. Your energy levels increase and you are able to feel less sluggish at every turn. This creates more stamina in you, more energy in you and the ability to understand yourself when your resistance to work comes in. When you have all these you are in good physical shape to do what it takes and perform maximally in whatever you need to do to meet your goals.

Step 2 Eat Healthy

The next step is that you should keep your body healthy by eating right. The popular saying *"you are what you eat"* is not a joke. It really is true. If you eat well, and you eat healthy, your body is going to be in peak performance. That's what you are looking for. You want the body to be able to respond to the mind whenever it needs it.

Eating healthy doesn't mean that you go out and start changing your diets to something that is a fad. You don't need to become a vegan if you don't want to. You just need to do what is healthy. Eat healthy portions of well-prepared food. Take away all the junk that comes from fast food and processed food.

When I went off processed foods I didn't realize how addicted to it my body was until the third day of giving it up and my body started craving the salt and the fats. Manufactured food companies know exactly what your body craves and they give you exactly that so that you get hooked. There is a balance of sugar, fat, and salt that if you use that ratio, you will have customers back for more every time. Big companies know this and they use it to the maximum, but that ruins your body and sometimes messes with the brain. None of this is worth you losing out on being able to move mountains.

Remember, you are not looking to just get up and survive, you looking to explode and thrive.

Step 3 Balance

Remember that you have dual purposes. You never want to get into a position where you favor one at the expense of the other. If you are a pizza delivery guy that uses your car to deliver your pizzas, aside from you, the thing that is important is your car. Without your car, you can't get the pizzas to your customer.

Just like that, your body is the seat of your soul. Without your body, you can't succeed in this world. You need to be able to balance your priorities and you need to pay as much attention to your body and your family as you do to the effort that you need to succeed.

The first three steps talk about your body and how to balance that, the next three steps are about how you bring massive action to your inspiration.

Step 4 Know Your Stuff

Knowing your stuff is not about how much knowledge you have, ironically, it's about how much you do and how consistent you are. You need to get up and do things and when you notice that there is a mistake, you rectify that mistake and move on. The changes to the mistake you make are different from what we referred to as failure in my book 'Fail Your Way to Success'.

When you do not have the faintest idea of something but you feel inspired to do it, do not be discouraged from attempting it. Knowing your stuff doesn't mean that you go and learn before you start - it means learning while you are performing that action.

Keep yourself open to learning while you perform such action because that is the best way to achieve the best results. When you consign yourself to thinking that everything can be gotten from books, you fail to understand a vital lesson of life which is that the best learning can be found in practice and not theory. So understand and accept the fact that you are going to make mistakes. You might as well jump in and start now and fail early so that you can learn more.

You should not be afraid of starting just because you don't know everything. I can guarantee you this, you could spend a lifetime learning from books but you will still make mistakes when you get in the ring. If everyone who learned from books was guaranteed success, then there would be too many successful people around. Knowledge is the key but not the prerequisite. You learn on the job and you become fearless through that!

Step 5 Clarity

Be crystal clear about what you are going after. If you are inspired, you will know exactly what you are going after. Many people start off without knowing what they are going after exactly and that is a huge potential for failure, which is not the kind you want. You can fail to learn but not fail because you have a lack of clarity where you are going. The Wright Brothers started out to make a flying contraption. They knew exactly what they wanted and they got exactly that - they didn't end up with a grass cutter. They knew what the final objective and product would be.

The same goes for Thomas Edison. Even Alexander the Great knew what he was going after. Edison didn't just start out fiddling around and miss ten thousand times before stumbling onto a game changer. It never works that way. There must always be clarity of objective derived from your inspiration.

If you are truly inspired you will have the clarity you need to be totally confident of what you are embarking on. If you can be clear about that, then your purpose is crystal clear and your efforts will never be wasted.

People who are serial losers make a tragic mistake here. They take the first part of the advice, they put in massive action but they do it behind uninspired ideas. That is a sure recipe for failure. Don't do that.

If you do not have the full inspiration of the universe in your back pocket, don't commit to such massive action because you will set yourself up for something that is nothing short of a catastrophic fail.

To have clarity, you need to be able to meditate and understand your purpose. One of the things that Steve Jobs did, that not many people are aware of, is that he was a student of meditation. He used to read books on the subject and he was fascinated with how such efforts to meditate and understand a vision can bring about massive potentials in life. His ability to be inspired and his ability to apply massive action is what brought about the iPhone in my pocket, the iPad on my desk, and the iMac that I am writing these words on.

In the process, he reaped the rewards of reaching greatness that many fail to enjoy. His successes were many and his mark on the world still shows. If it wasn't for him, so many industries would have been left without any impact. It was his inspiration, his clarity of final objective, and the massive action that got the Apple brand to where it is today.

Step 6 Keep Moving

Momentum is a form of energy that most people do not get. I look at it sometimes, as free energy. Once you start moving, momentum is already on your side. As long as you have the clarity of vision and you have the inspiration of the universe, do not be afraid to use momentum to carry part of your efforts. While you keep applying massive action, you can be sure that some of the weight will be carried by this momentum. However, you have to be aware of the levels you have reached.

In the event that you lose awareness or mindfulness, you may lose control of the momentum and that could take you down the wrong path. As long as inspiration, mindfulness, and massive action are steaming on ahead, go ahead and let that momentum work in your favor.

There is a lot to be said about rhythm and momentum. Rhythm is the beat to which you move. In the case of massive action, your action should be one that is constant and consistent. This aids in your momentum. If you are not consistent, you will not have a reliable momentum.

As inspired as you are, an improper rhythm will derail your efforts by shortcutting your momentum. You need to be able to get the constant movement going.

A good way to do that is to have a disciplined schedule.

Disciplined Schedule

A disciplined schedule goes a long way in advancing your actions. However, let me just make this clear, your disciplined schedule should leave room for some quality free time and it should be one that is balanced. You can't spend all your time working and leave your family out of the picture.

A disciplined schedule is spending time at work and engaging in every means to achieve success. You have no time to surf, no time to chat or shoot the breeze. You are on a mission when you take on the decision to advance with massive action. Every moment you are breathing is a moment in the present that is creating a foundation for the future. You need to appreciate each moment and do what you can in that moment without wasting it.

As a foundation of a disciplined schedule, you should create one day where you need to unplug. In my personal life, I am surrounded by technology in all forms. The social media, the hardware, the blogs and even my news and groceries are online. I am connected in so many ways to so many people that if I don't engage in what I ought to do, it would all get to be too much.

What do I do? Well, once a week, beginning at midnight on Saturday, I totally unplug. No TV, no phone, no email. Nothing electronic touches my life for 24 hours. It is an electronic Sabbath day.

I started this eight years ago when I started getting too much of everything fed to me in real time, and this slowly began to crowd out my own intuition and my senses. By unplugging, I allowed myself to come back on Monday with a new perspective. I was fully recharged and fully alert. In the beginning, it felt strange to just unplug and do nothing. But I realized that, by unplugging, I was actually recharging my soul and refining my inspiration.

As part of a disciplined schedule, I also take Saturdays off and spend it with my family, catching up, being with them and just soaking them up. We spend the full weekend together and when we get back to the work week, each of us is able to fully dive into whatever we were doing.

My entire family practices massive action. Whether it's school, work or leisure, we do everything to the best of our abilities and capabilities.

***

Chapter 5 Managing Output with Inspiration

As with anything that you plan and carry out, you need some form of feedback mechanism to make sure that you are getting to the place you want to get to without losing your focus and objectives. You need to be able to look at the work you are doing and assess it with benchmarks that you set up in the beginning.

When it comes to massive action and using momentum to drive actions and ideas that arise from your inspiration, you need to look back and refine the ideas that you originally had. If you look at the ideas you came up with, and the outcome of the project, and they seem to be similar or better than the projections you had before the project, you are on the right track. But if you look back and they are way below the starting standard you intended to reach, you need to go back to the drawing board and ask yourself why. All these steps are pretty self-evident and you need to fit them into your schedule.

Mind you, the reason you do this is not to doubt the original plan or idea but to make sure you don't get gremlins in the system and that you are where you are supposed to be. The last thing you want is to race to the finish line only to find that you are way off course.

By keeping an eye on your present position, you will always be able to automatically benchmark it to your inspiration, and that will allow you to make corrections and alterations when you think necessary. But more often than not, the real benefit of doing this is to keep the objective in mind. It's a tool to keep all things on even ground.

Cultivate Asking

There are two kinds of inquiry that we can broadly categorize everything into. The first is the inquiry that you make at the higher level of vibration. We've talked about that all through the course of this book.

There are other kinds of inquiries that you should cultivate as well and they bring with them two benefits; One on the practical plane of existence; and the other on the psychological plane of existence.

The first is the kind of asking that you do at the physical level. Whenever you do not know something, take the time to ask. Whether it is directions to a certain destination, or it's advice on how to do something. Always cultivate the habit of asking when you don't know something.

By doing this, you will begin to understand that whatever you need is out there. Someone out there knows something that you need to know, and he or she could help you in figuring out what you need to figure out and solve your puzzle.

The second thing you begin to learn is that your ego begins to retreat and you learn to trust other people's opinions. *'Man is not an island of his own'*. This popular saying helps put this point into perspective. When your mind starts to figure that it gets more benefit from asking, your psyche starts to reevaluate its misguided ego.

"Pride always comes before the fall", or so the saying goes. The pride, which this text refers to, is the ego that is inflated within all of us. When you learn to ask, it becomes second nature and you start to make it a habit that spreads across all areas of your life.

When in Doubt, Ask

The beauty about this universe - and I am not talking about space and the planets that inhabit it. Rather, I am talking about the energy of all things that occupy it. From the nothingness of everything to the elements and the phenomena, and most importantly the underlying energy that gives life to all things. The beauty of this universe is that it is here to give you whatever you desire so that you can make this world better than the state you met it.

The universe can and will give you whatever you ask for, even if you are not suited to take advantage of it. It will give you the answers you need and give you the strength you need to answer the tough situations that come up in your quest for greatness. It will even give you a step by step instruction manual to get you from zero to hero, if you just do one simple thing – ask.

Much more than that, if you ever come to a fork in the road and you are in doubt, go ahead and ask. The gift of Inquiry is the greatest gift that we are given, but unfortunately, it is also one of the most under-used.

You came across this book because you decided you needed help in some area of your life. The answer you need is in here somewhere, or at least it's somewhere that this book will lead to. If you asked for it, it will come. It's as simple as that.

Have you ever considered what happens when two people ask for the same thing? The universe does not play favorites and as I mentioned before, the universe answers with the presentation of opportunities. The person who makes the best of his opportunities wins.

Just a Few More Steps

When you seem to be failing in whatever you are given, especially when you asked for it, and you are working on it, and the more you work on it, the more, you need to realize that you are just a few steps away from breakthrough and dig in deeper.

When you are on the road to success, the one thing you need to remember is that you need to focus on the level you are currently in, if you are not hitting pay dirt, that's ok. You can stop and ask for inspiration, but keep applying massive action to what you are doing.

Can you imagine if Orville Wright decided that he was going to stop just because he couldn't solve the weight and balance issue of the Wright Flyer because it would topple over every time they launched it? How would you get to Aspen next winter if planes weren't invented?

Every single invention that you touch, from the device you use to call your family, to the car you drive and all the hundreds of different bells and whistles in the car including Marconi's radio invention, Ford's mass production idea, and hundreds of other ideas that were the inspiration to someone who took it and worked hard at it until it became of use to you and me.

***

Chapter 6 Believing

It takes time for people to learn how to believe in themselves and while some eventually figure it out, many seem to fall by the wayside and never apply this vital tool in the quest to live excellent lives. They are then unable to become successful in their endeavors.

The problem is that such people rely more on hope than on asking and acting. Hope has its place in getting to the finish line, but personally, I prefer belief than hope. Once I start something, it never occurs to me that nothing but the outcome I have intended, will come to fruition. I believe in my heart and with my soul that I will eventually prevail. It is a certainty in my mind, not a doubt.

This has been a guiding principle in all my adult career that I would always do what is necessary to get what I envision to be the final outcome.

Belief is a complicated concept. Not because it is complex on its own, but because all the descriptions of it, and all the misunderstandings that are attached to it by secular and religious commentators alike have muddied the waters of the people's knowledge.

We will dive deeper into the topic in the next book in the series, but for now, you must get a bit of an introduction to it because asking and believing are two very important aspects of success that are the products of freewill.

When we examined the other elements of success that were presented in the first three books, a different tone from this was noticeable. The art of failing talks about the way to learn from 'trial by error' and allowing failure to be your true guide. Discipline talks about doing what is necessary; while meditating talks about the elements you need to develop your inspiration and then to go after your success.

But this book about asking has an element of individuality to it. You can ask for anything you want. It is a question of freewill that comes into play. In meditation, you do what you have to do to come into contact with the universe. In failing, you have no choice but to get up and try again if you want to succeed. In discipline, you don't have a choice either if you want to succeed. But in asking, you are given freewill.

Yes, there is a way to meditate on what to ask for, you are more predisposed to succeed at some things more than others by virtue of your environment and your experience, but you can still decide to engage in the things you fancy while succeeding in them. The universe will still give you the opportunity to make it happen, but the difference is that you have the freedom to make whatever you want it to be, from your life.

The same goes for the topic of believing. Believing is not just accepting what you're told, but what you want. If you truly believe a thing, you are that much closer to making that thing happen. Belief is not blind acceptance of everything that people say. Belief is not about 'buying it', rather, it is about knowing that you are meant for greatness and that everything that happens in your life is a step to that final destination.

***

Conclusion

You need to remember that success is a serious affair. You can't take it for granted and you can't neglect the various elements that go into brewing it. You need to reflect on what your affinity to success is, and you need to examine your motivations. If you are motivated by the rewards that come at the end of a successful venture, you are going to be able to get those rewards, but they won't be the kind of success that you have the potential of achieving.

At the same time, don't allow the fact that success is serious detract you or distract you from going after it. Never be discouraged or fazed by the prospect of taking the bull by the horn. It may be serious, but it's not more than you can handle. Most people think they are suffering when they begin to strive for something and often do not know that suffering is a mental state and not a tangible feeling. Suffering is when you don't know what you are capable of and you are put to the test. I want you to understand that you have the potential in you and it is possible to achieve anything and everything you can imagine or anything and everything that you are inspired to accomplish. You owe it to yourself to be able to pick up the mantle and go for the success that you are capable of.

For now, you need to be able to know how to vibrate, and if you know how to do that, get started. If you don't, you are more than welcome to pick up any book about meditation and mindfulness, or pick up the one in this series, and you will start to understand that meditation is just the vibration you need to be at so that the desires in your heart are sent out into the universe and the gifts and opportunities that come back to you are because of what you asked for.

The universe does not understand English, Polish, Russian or Chinese. It probably doesn't even understand Martian (or any other extra-terrestrial language). The universe understands your vibrations. When you meditate, you enter that vibration and you become at one with the energy that is at the center of all things. That's how you ask.

But you also take your request and translate it into your spoken language. If it is exactly what you want, then you should feel the thrill at the very sound of it. You will feel the ground move when you pinpoint exactly what you want, but you can't do it if you are not at peace and you are not aware of the uniqueness of the art of meditation.

Peace and awareness come from the ability to be mindful and to be focused. Interestingly enough, those are the two things you need to be in a state of meditation. When you are in this state, what you need to ask for is that the paths to success become clearer for you to tread on. That means you start to understand your path. Some people call this "The Calling". Some say it is faith. For the longest time, I refused to believe in predestined paths and what I am meant to do is dictated by the universe or by the divine. However, I soon realized that the notion of destiny is not about a predestined path, but it is one which is created by our own actions.

Who we become in life is a function of what we do, the kinds of experiences we allow ourselves to have, and the kinds of mindsets we form over time. That, in turn, bequeaths to us a set of experiences and skills that automatically make us good or better at some particular thing. When we are predisposed to something, we automatically become qualified to do that and have a higher chance of being able to succeed at something that utilizes that skill. This is a simplified way of laying it out, although it does strike at the heart of the matter. But the thing that you cannot fathom or predict is what you know and what can be open to you. For that, only the universe can help.

If you are not sure what to ask for, then the best way is for you to actually meditate. It's a way for you to ask the universe to show you what areas you could possibly be good at and succeed.

Remember that the opportunities you see from that point onwards can be classified into one of three categories. It can either be exactly what you need, or it can be what you would like, but when it comes at a time that it is more of a distraction than an aid, it is a pure distraction that is not worth your effort and time.

When I first started the art meditation, I used to get a lot of false positives. It really took me for a ride. I was getting so many opportunities, and at first, I thought that it was great. I never had that many opportunities knock on my door. Then I started to realize that even though the opportunities were aplenty, true success was nowhere to be found.

The more I meditated, I realized I could feel that I was all over the place in terms of what I wanted and what I wanted to succeed at. So finally, I narrowed it down to one. It was a highly iterative process that went from cogitation to meditation then back to cogitation again. In time, the two started to yield complementary paths. I could feel the energy from just looking at the right direction and the correct path. It felt different from all the other so-called "opportunities" that came by only to knock me off my horse.

Once I knew what it felt like, I knew what to look for. That has not let me down since that moment of realization. Every time I did something, I always knew exactly what followed next, and each time I committed myself to a certain task, I committed fully. It involved putting everything that I had into achieving such tasks without being distracted.

In time, you will be able to do it too. You need to be able to set your sights and you need to ask. Asking is the first step in aligning all the forces that are at your disposal. If you don't ask, you won't be able to get it.

Even the bible talks about asking. You may even know it well. Matthew 7:7 says, **"Ask and you shall receive"** It is true, and I am here to tell you that if you truly desire it; If you truly believe it (and I will show you what belief is in the next book); and if you meditate and vibrate at the frequency of the universe, you will get exactly what you ask for.

***

Epilogue

Do not confuse success with achievement. Everyone makes that mistake. We all know how to achieve things. We set a goal, we undergo the process, and we achieve the goal: Not a big deal. We learned to do that in kindergarten. We all have achievements to point to in the past and we can all build on them. Being a success story, which is very different from just succeeding at something or achieving something, is serious business.

It requires the desire to do something phenomenal. It requires the inspiration from the universe that we attract and the 'know how' to recognize. It requires the initiation of the process of searching for knowledge and the buildup of the ability to make it real. It requires the discipline to pursue and to transform intangible plans and ideas into workable ones with immediate effectiveness.

You can achieve a task by following instructions, but to be successful, you need to bind your mind, body, and soul together in a seamless continuum. You need to be inspired, disciplined, energized and sharp all at the same time. You need to be proactive, tireless and adopt a fearless disposition all the time.

We all want to succeed in life even though it is at different levels. We are not always sure why we get that desire, but we do. We think success is localized and relevant only over the next quarter or just in our neighborhood or, at best, among our circle of associates. After all that, we go to bed at night wondering where we are in life and how that present condition seems insufficient. On the other hand, we are perfectly content with our weekly sports night, our annual mid-budget vacations, or TV dinners, a mortgaged house, and our leased vehicles. We think that's success.

News Flash! It's not.

Whatever you're doing does not amount to success until your handiwork has an impact on the world. Unless you are adding to this world something that inspires you and that which you've worked at bringing it to life which now makes a positive difference - you're not a success. And as long as you are not a success, you will continue to be rewarded according to your current level. The true reward of success is deep and peaceful contentment. There will always be something missing inside you if you do not make success your life.

There are three things you need to be intimately close to when you want to make success your way of life; the first is that you need to find your inspiration. The second is that you need to build the discipline to convert inspiration into massive actions.

There are two additional items that are grounded in freewill that you have to think long and hard before you do, and they are the; compunction to ask and the strength to believe. These two elements bestow the control of your destiny in your hands.

All that is covered in the next book, *Believe Your Way to Success*. In it, you will get to understand how the most unexpected individuals climb to the pinnacle of success. Look at men with innate disabilities that dare the odds and believe that they can do more than those who seem to have everything going for them.

Between your understanding of the purpose of asking and your eventual understanding of believing, you will indeed be able to change this world to suit your desires.

As you come to the end of this book, remember that you should go back and read it again. You should reflect on your own life and apply the words that you find here to the life that you've lived.

May you find your inspiration, and may you change the world with your success!

***

Make sure to check out the rest of the books in this series:

Fail Your Way to Success: The Definitive Guide to Failing Forward and Learning How to Extract the Greatness Within - Why Failing is an Integral Part of Success and Why You Should Never Fear it

https://www.amazon.com/dp/B0738WDK6W

Discipline Your Way to Success: The Definitive Guide to Success Through Self-Discipline - Why Self-Discipline is Crucial to Your Success Story and How to Take Control Over Your Thoughts and Actions

https://www.amazon.com/dp/B0741FMCBX

Meditate Your Way to Success: The Definitive Guide to Mindfulness, Focus and Meditation - How Meditation is an Integral Part of Success and Why You Should Get Started Now

https://www.amazon.com/dp/B073ZMCHQJ

Believe Your Way to Success: The Definitive Guide to Believing and Your Path to Success How Believing Takes You from Where You are to Where You Want to Be

https://www.amazon.com/dp/B0747N14KF

www.ingramcontent.com/pod-product-compliance
Lightning Source LLC
Chambersburg PA
CBHW021135300426
44113CB00006B/441